WORDPLAY

GROUNDHOG

PRESENTS

Published By
Wordplay Groundhog
WordPlayGroundhog.com

TRACTORS

FOUND ON THE FARM

A WORDPLAY GROUNDHOG BOOK

FARMS ARE THE BEST PLACE TO FIND A TRACTOR.

BIG AND SMALL.
FARMS HAVE THEM ALL.

RED TRACTORS.

BLUE TRACTORS.

OLD TRACTORS.

NEW TRACTORS.
(IT'S TRUE. BULLDOZERS ARE TRACTORS TOO!)

ORANGE TRACTORS.

GREEN TRACTORS.

MUDDY TRACTORS.

CLEAN TRACTORS.

TRACTORS IN
THE MORNING.

TRACTORS GOING LEFT.

TRACTORS
GOING RIGHT.

TRACTORS PLANTING SEEDS IN THE GROUND.

TRACTORS DIGGING UNDER THE GROUND.

TRACTORS WITH GOATS
AND COWS AROUND.

TRACTORS MAKING
TRACTOR SOUNDS.

VROOOOOM!

TRACTORS IN THE SUN.

TRACTORS IN THE SNOW.

TRACTORS IN THE DIRT.

TRACTORS IN THE GRASS.
READY TO MOW.

FARMS ARE GREAT. BUT YOU CAN FIND TRACTORS ANYPLACE.

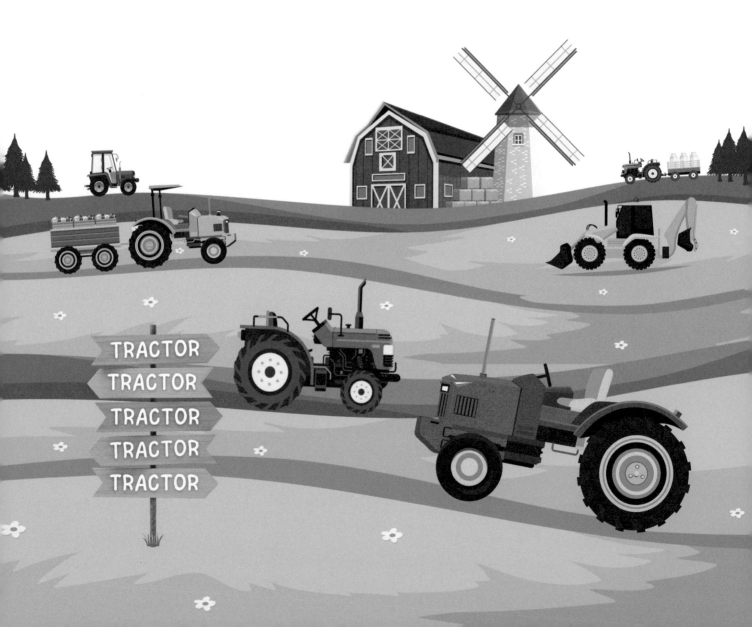

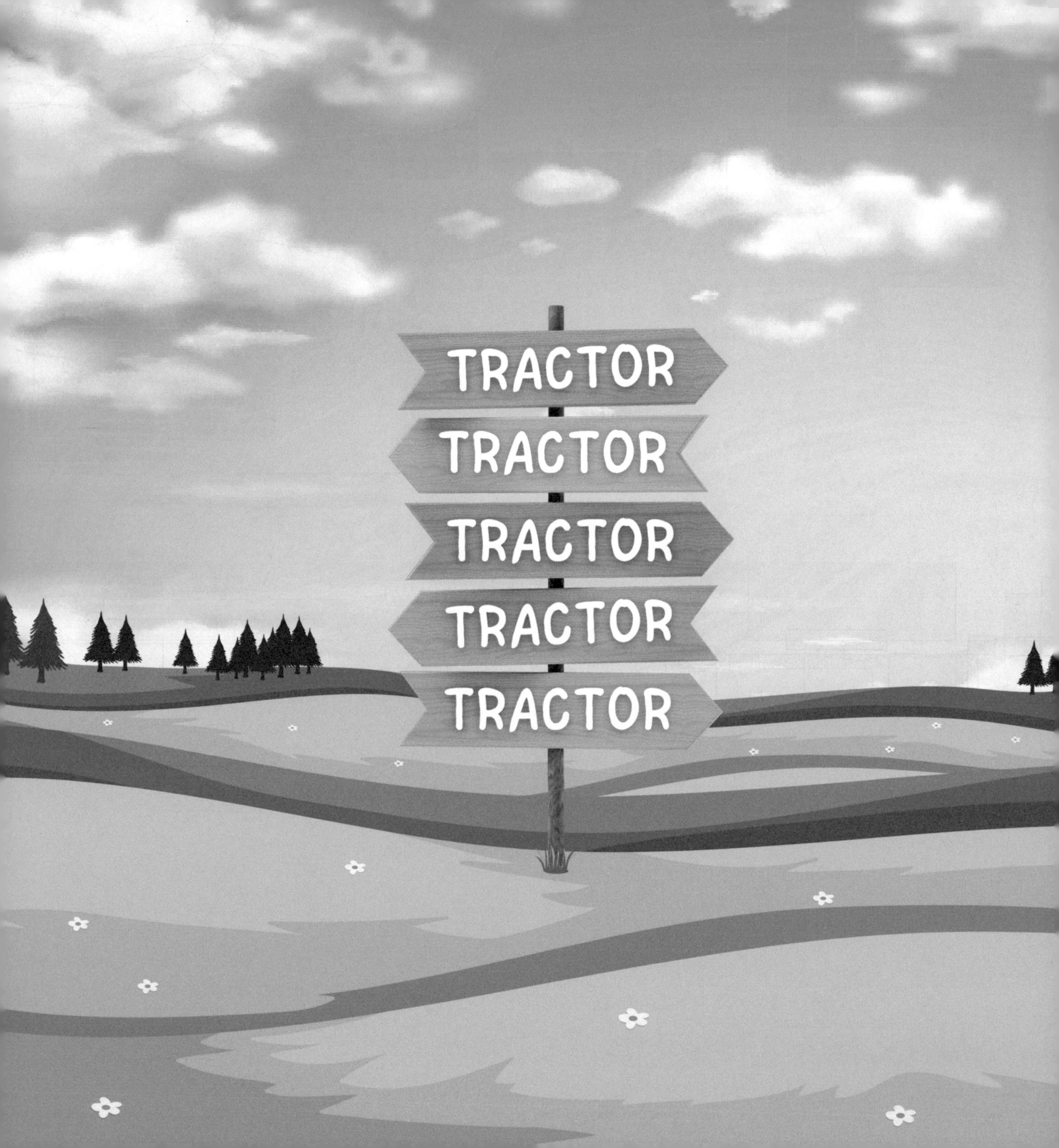
TRACTOR
TRACTOR
TRACTOR
TRACTOR
TRACTOR

More Books For Kids
By Wordplay Groundhog

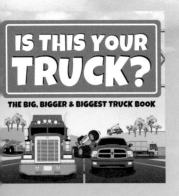
IS THIS YOUR TRUCK?
THE BIG, BIGGER & BIGGEST TRUCK BOOK

HOW TO MAKE A PENGUIN LAUGH

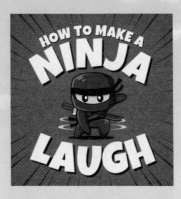
HOW TO MAKE A NINJA LAUGH

HOW TO MAKE AN ASTRONAUT LAUGH

WORLD CHAMPION SOCCER JOKES

WORLD CHAMPION VOLLEYBALL JOKES

HOW TO MAKE A PIRATE LAUGH

UNICORNS MAKE THE BEST CLASS PETS!
A WORDPLAY GROUNDHOG BOOK.

HOW TO MAKE A LION LAUGH

HOW TO MAKE A UNICORN LAUGH

HOW TO MAKE AN ELEPHANT LAUGH

HO-HO-HO-LARIOUS CHRISTMAS JOKES

WORDPLAYGROUNDHOG.COM